I LOVE YOU GREATER THAN SPACE!

By Lucy Dunn Blount

Illustrated by Mary Barwick

Your sister in Christ,
Lucy.

authorHOUSE®

AuthorHouse™
1663 Liberty Drive
Bloomington, IN 47403
www.authorhouse.com
Phone: 1-800-839-8640

Published by AuthorHouse 3/14/2013

ISBN: 978-1-4817-1275-0 (sc)
ISBN: 978-1-4817-1276-7 (e)

Library of Congress Control Number: 2013902304

This book is printed on acid-free paper.

Because of the dynamic nature of the Internet, any web addresses or links contained
in this book may have changed since publication and may no longer be valid.

The views expressed in this work are solely those of the author and do not necessarily reflect
the views of the publisher, and the publisher hereby disclaims any responsibility for them.

"HE HAS TAKEN ME TO THE BANQUET HALL

AND HIS BANNER OVER ME IS LOVE"

Song of Solomon 2:4

To my love and soulmate, Pablo
"You will always change the world of everyone you touch."
You profoundly touch and change mine.
You are such a *Gift* and I thank the Lord for you.
Lucia

Preface

"In sorrow great joy can come forth."

That was the statement proclaimed by our visiting minister ring her sermon. For me, it was a gift of answered prayer. hank You, Lord."

You see, Precious Pilgrim, for months I've sensed a gentle ssing on my spirit to publish these old writings in book m. "But why?" That was my unresolved question. I just ıldn't understand the need, but that nagging pressure ıtinued. I began to take tentative steps towards that goal, ıtinually praying, "Lord, if this is not of You, please block : way."

Re-reading, correcting, recording remained weighty moves ause of my attitude. It was as if I was carrying a heavy back- :k with that "question" stuffed inside. "Yes, Lord, but why?"

At the precise moment needed the perfect person would ne forth ~ Liz Griffin for typing, Julie Toffaletti for design- , Harry Moore for editing, Larry Griffin for sending. The ır remained open. One by one the sequential stepping ıes would appear as the faith walk continued.

This morning before church, I was sitting on a stool in my le closet with pen and paper. I knew it was now time to write ; Preface. Everything else had been done. I began: "We know t we have passed from death to life, because we love one ıther." 1 John 3:14. That was the scripture verse on my husband Paul's and my wedding announcement almost nine years ago. He was a widower; I, a widow. We saw and continu to see our love as a gift from the Lord. Paul is my best friend and soul mate. The last time I'd read these writings was out loud to him during our courting days. We were and are committed to completely sharing our life stories. These are just some of mine.

"But why?" Funny, I'd almost forgotten that age-old question. It's as if that humble forward motion had knocked a hole in my imaginary backpack. The "Yes, Lord" steps had taken control. That negative "but why?" question had its wind knocked out so that our Lord's Holy Spirit WIND could take charge.

And then the answer unexpectedly came:

"In sorrow great joy can come forth."

Amen. To God be the gl

ecious Pilgrim,

Before sending this work out, I've asked the Reverend Tom ard to make a few comments. He was one of Duncan's best ends. By God's grace, it was through their shared nversations that Duncan became a committed Christian.

Tom knew Duncan during the joyful season he shared with s late wife Betty and during the despairing one experienced er her death from cancer.

Tom and I met during my season of brokenness after a vorce from one of his college classmates. He and I were at-ndees at a Centering Prayer conference held in Sewanee, Ten-ssee. Tom was then chaplain for the University of the South.

That summer Duncan and I met. That fall we were arried. On returning the following summer to that mountain, e first couple we sought was Peggy and Tom. We felt com-lled to share our joy with them for we knew that they would n in our rejoicing and giving thanks and praise to our Father d for the gift of this new season of LOVE. They did.

That next summer, it was Tom's presence that fleshed t the comforting, supportive love of Jesus for me the night ncan died. I called. He came. I'll never forget his 6'6" pres-ce standing outside the entrance of the Emergency Room. at burdensome darkness seemed to become bearably lighter.

It was Tom that officiated at Betty and Duncan's marriage. vas Tom that officiated at Duncan's funeral held at the

Sewanee University Chapel. Later, on a misty, rainy, English-like morning, it was Tom, Peggy and I who interred his ashes the Monteagle Assembly's cemetery.

We continue to occasionally see each other when Tom directs Centering Prayer workshops at our church. I sense tha he once again joins me in rejoicing and giving thanks and praise for this new gift of LOVE ~ my husband, Paul Pressly M Cain, and I will soon be celebrating our ninth wedding anniversary.

Each LOVE is unique. Each LOVE is a gift. I humbly giv thanks to the Lord.

Now here's the Reverend Tom Ward:

"You can make me sit here, but you cannot make me believe anything." Those were the first words I remember hea ing Duncan MacLeod speak after our having gone through ot introductory social exchanges. Duncan had come for a requir premarital conversation because the woman he wanted to marry wished to be married in the church where she was a co municant and I was a priest. Two months and eight meetings later Duncan was able to affirm the Christian faith, and I hac been a privileged witness to his conversion. Duncan was able see and acknowledge that the God who raised Jesus from the dead had sent Betty Maney into his life.

Almost fifteen years later, I saw Duncan in love again. He and Lucy had met and married and were clearly entranced wi one another. This time Duncan needed no convincing that h had again been given a gift, for he had continued to grow in I

th over the years. Lucy had been grounded in the faith all of
r life.

Death is a central character in this story. Only months
er Duncan and Betty's wedding, she discovered that she had
ethal form of cancer, with the doctors giving her only a few
onths to live. That changed everything. While Duncan ful-
ed the duties of his position as an Oxford don, he focused
s immense energies on Betty and their life together, dividing
eir time between England and the United States, traveling,
ting, and tending to Betty's medical needs. It was a joy to be
their presence, and Betty lived many years longer than any-
e expected. (Her doctor called her longevity a miracle.) But
the end death came, as death always will.

Death came to Duncan as well after only 623 days of
arried life with Lucy. What follows is a partial record of those
ys, their courtship, and the grief that followed Duncan's
ath. This is another love story with the Risen Lord Jesus at its
nter: love is stronger than death. Lucy has now married Paul,
d Paul makes a place for Duncan. He had lost his first wife to
ath as well.

For years this intricate narrative has reminded me of an-
ner transatlantic love affair (in fact another Oxford-America
mance): that of C.S. Lewis and Joy Davidman, which many
us know through the book and the movie "Shadowlands."
common theme here is the Christian faith with the Paschal
ystery at its center. God sends men and women to each other
embodiments of God's love. Death separates them on this
rth, but God brings them and all of us to a deeper, transcen-
nt relation in the Communion of Saints.

Adam and Eve, Dante and Beatrice, C.S. Lewis and Joy Davidman, Duncan and Betty, Duncan and Lucy – the love between a man and a woman is a central way that God has spoken and continues to speak. Duncan knew this love twice. As Lucy tells us in her introduction, the three works that comprise this book bear witness to the love they shared and to the God who is love. It is Lucy's hope and mine that her words m speak to you of the love of God and encourage you on your own journey in Christ.

Tom Ward

Introduction

cious One,

I want so desperately to be able to capture this experience,
 "synchronicity of Duncan the Cloud," but how does one
 such a thing? How can one put into words an unworldly
 perience? It doesn't compute or seem rational. You can't
 nspose or translate; at least I've found it extremely difficult.
 at's why I've been slipping into Haiku-like poetry. That
 cipline seems to help me fine-tune and pare down the
 perience into a more manageable one. But goodness, I can't
 end the rest of my life trying to communicate through
 iku-talk about a dead language!

If we were living in the world of Greek mythology or
 ivalry or romance as opposed to this computer age, I believe
 ere would be more respect and reverence for the unexplain-
 e, the incomprehensible, the mysterious, the synchronicity
 life like the one Duncan and I experienced.

Joseph Jaworski says in his book *The Inner Path of
 adership*:

"We've all had those perfect moments, when things
come together in an almost unbelievable way, when events
that could never be predicted, let alone controlled,
remarkably seem to guide us along our path. The closest
I've come to finding a word for what happens in these

moments is synchronicity. C.G. Jung's classic 'Synchonicity: an acausal connecting principal' defines synchronicity as a meaningful coincidence of two or more events, where something other than the probability of chance is involved. In the beautiful flow of these moments it seems as if we are being helped by hidden hands."

Yes, As a Christian, I see these hands as our Father God's

The above was written in Duncan's office in St. Catherine's College, Oxford University, England. While waiting for him to return from a meeting, I was trying to capture the wonder of our world. Ah, the wonder of our world – all was and all continues to be a gift.

In this book, you will find three works. "**Soaring Songs,**" haiku-style poetry, was written and given to Duncan in celebration of our first Christmas together. Haiku is the Japanese form of poetry wherein the number of syllables in each line is five, then seven, then five, completing the stanza. "**Duncan Doodle Dog**" was written very soon after Duncan's unexpected death from a heart attack. It was written to my grandchildren to help comfort them. "**Ta, Gorgeous**" ("ta" is an endearing term for thank you) is haiku-style poetry written during the months following Duncan's death.

We had 623 days of absolute marital bliss. As I said, all was and all continues to be a gift. Duncan's love fleshed out the Love of Jesus for me. We ended each night with Evening Prayer and the thanksgiving declaration to our Father God of "Grateful, grateful!" These were Duncan's last words.

hey continue to reverberate in my spirit.

It is my prayer that by your joining Duncan and me in this very personal, eternal, synchronized dance of love, you will find words of encouragement for your own dance. And also join us celebrating the truthfully wise, boundless words spoken by my four-year-old grandson, Jud:

"I love you greater than space!"

Your sister in Christ,
Lucy

P.S. I'd like to thank my precious daughter Stuart for all of her help in editing and designing this book. You are and have always been a grand gift, too.

Soaring Songs

Duncan Doodle-Dog

"Ta, Gorgeous"

Table of Contents

Soaring Songs

Delightful Details

"A room with a view."
Your eyes met mine in the crowd
As a magnet draws.

A birthing begins.
Hope seems to flutter inside,
Healing brokenness.

Your England address
Only miles from the convent.
What are the chances?

One in a million
Or even greater than that?
A coincidence?

Chance meeting, three times
Invitation to your porch.
A drive by "thank you."

"Might you write?" You did,
Telling me about yourself.
I asked. You complied.

It was a treasure,
A gift of intimacy
Thoughtfully given.

A planned rendezvous.
An Atlanta dinner date.
A kiss of greeting.

You draw me forward
Into a new beginning.
The chrysalis cracks.

Gently encouraged,
Softly you share your story,
Listening to mine.

I'm dreaming again,
"Like visions of sugar plums"
Twirling in my mind.

Singing, joyful soul,
Prancing, dancing with delight.
A resurrection.

"Fear not. All is well."
Nothing more is required.
A walk is enough.

A smile is enough,
More than enough, each was grand.
The sun is shining.

I'm forward facing.
Never a Lot-wifeish stance.
I'm rainbow hopeful.

Future plans? Who knows?
"All is well and all is well."
This precious present.

Duncan John MacLeod,
Happy Birthday and thank you.
Joint celebration.

October 7, 200

From Bridges to Plateau

Heart brimming with joy,
Intimacy of two days
Filled with emotions.

You touched me deeply.
An awakening begins.
Lucy might come forth.

Verdant horizons
Fertile possibilities.
New worlds might await.

I can still smell you.
The warmth of you does excite.
Hugs and hands twining.

The glorious views.
Waterfalls, rock formations,
Swimming holes, mushrooms.

Blue eyes, strong back, smiles.
You opened my door and heart
With gentle respect.

Oh, how good it felt.
More than in 29 years.
Your presence blessed me.

A road poem by Frost.
Exciting choices to choose.
Words carved in the bridge.

A lingering hug.
You said it was a good fit.
Content, I concur.

A penny to toss,
Closing my eyes on the bridge.
A wish and a prayer.

Porch and sofa sit.
Tuna tomato sandwich.
Classical music.

Sharing life stories.
Twirling, dancing, delightful.
Playing back and forth.

Two exquisite days.
"Magical." Yes, I agree.
Filling me with hope.

An angel given,
A Sewanee guardian
With yellow roses.

"You are wonderful."
Thank you for such a goodbye.
Reverberating.

I feel like a child
Anticipating newness.
Anxious to grow up.

As if a virgin
Scared but ready to blossom,
To become myself.

Thwart seeds of interests
Never allowed to flourish.
Dormant yet not dead.

I need a tutor.
Might you be willing to teach?
I'm willing to learn.

Might you need one, too?
My imagination soars.
Possibilities.

Happy Birthday --
Is this scary or what?
October 7, 2000

A Doxology

(I awoke at 12:45 AM at the convent with this
Doxology singing through me)

All praise to You, Lord.
All honor, glory and might.
I adore You, Lord.

I worship You, Lord.
You rescued me from the mire.
Tenderly picked up.

You caressed my soul.
A "Gilead balm" applied,
Soothing every wound.

Healing unknown hurts.
You loved me into wholeness.
New freshness appears.

Areas of growth
As if a river flowing.
New tributaries.

Wobbly on my legs,
I'm like a newborn filly
Gaining strength from You.

Your blessings galore
Are too numerous to count.
More than stars above.

Constant Companion
Incomprehensible Love.
You, ardent Lover.

I cannot express.
Words seem so inadequate.
My feelings toward You.

God omnipotent
Omniscient, omnipresent.
Father, Son, Spirit.

Triune God, love me?
As if Your most precious bride.
"Lord, how can this be?"

Mary's ancient quest
Seems appropriate to ask.
"Lord, I'm unworthy."

Is what I declare.
But You do awesomely love.
It is Your nature.

Stomach is knotted.
I need to prostrate myself,
To fall on my face.

Setting all things right.
Another captive set free.
Un-caged butterfly.

Brilliant colored wings.
Empowered to do Your will.
Fragile, gossamer.

Lord, may I become
The creature You had in mind,
Your total design.

I am a sinner,
Prideful, self-centered, glutton.
But, but You love me

Lord and I love You.
Pitiful lamb that I am,
Little heart growing.

May I become more?
Loving You wholeheartedly.
More of You, less me.

Good Nig

Saints

Their lives become praise.
Every moment set apart.
Up, down, all around.

Two Roads Converged

Planning my exit
Take a Frosterian turn,
A less-traveled road.

Here comes "Mary Clare,"
A Sister extraordinaire.
She'll build a convent.

Tucked in the back woods.
Nestled all saintly and sure.
Alabama bound.

Lord Jesus, forgive.
You are the Savior, not me.
Such a work is Yours.

I'd look good in brown.
No more rollers or makeup.
Get rid of the stuff.

Clothes, jewels, furniture,
Heavy houses, boats, all toys.
Vamoose and goodbye.

Say "bye" to the kids,
Give hugs and kisses to grans.
They'd know where I was.

Stuck at Camp McDowell
Doing the Daily Office,
 "Holier than thou."

Wow! Wait, whoa, hold it.
Thank You, dear Lord Jesus Christ.
You blew this dream out.

It was mine, not Yours.
I'd go run and hide secure,
A prideful escape.

You had other plans.
On the Cumberland Plateau
A man with blue eyes.

A glance that did stick.
Freeland met Long Hanborough.
"Chance meeting," they'd say?

No, I don't think so.
It's too grand to imagine.
Years came together.

Five to be exact.
Lord, You are my Protector.
You took care of me.

When I didn't know,
A convent and Michaela
Came to my rescue.

Rescued from the mire,
Lord, You tenderly plucked out.
Placed on solid ground.

God spoke so clearly.
"You've done all you could - detach."
I did. Lord sustained.

Now, where do we go?
Heavens, I don't have a clue!
I'm dreaming galore.

Duncan, that is grand.
It is flat miraculous.
I'm floating in air.

I'm alive again,
Pulsating with energy -
Anticipating.

Please don't be afraid.
I'll now quit writing this stuff,
I can now speak prose.

I can slow me down.
I can relish this moment,
This time, place and space.

"Be-er and do-er."
You said that was what I was.
Now integration.

Time to become one.
Develop both sides of me.
Become more Lucy.

Now that's enough stuff.
Sorry for this spilling out,
Insightful for me.

Soon you will arrive.
I must stop and get ready
For an adventure.

If this is too much,
I'll understand completely.
You've given the gift.

I will cherish it.
Hope has resurfaced once more.
I thought it was dead.

But no, two roads met,
Freeland and Long Hanborough.
Each kissed life lightly.

And I proclaim,
Thanks!
October 7, 2000,
Your birthday and mine too!

In Love

In the midst of love
Languid, lipid, flowing love
Encircling me.

A warm mist of light
Ever so gently falling
Envelopes softly.

Oct. 10, 2000
Day before he proposed.

"Duncan the Cloud," I love you.

Evening Prayer and After
New College Chapel, Oxford

I feel your presence.
Every nerve of my body
Cries for more of you.

A pulsing hand held.
My side stands touching your side
Quietly, together.

Evening prayer reverence.
My heart aches from ecstasy.
Fathomless beauty.

"Ta" for such a gift,
Ethereal sights and sounds,
A desire fulfilled.

Shared experience.
Do you know what a blessing?
Richness multiplied.

To look in your eyes
And see delightful pleasure
Reflecting my mood.

Praying together,
Union of words lifted up,
Yearning realized.

"Be equally yoked."
It has been my heart's desire
For such a long time.

Lazarus comes forth,
His bindings are taken off.
You are taking mine.

Slowly you unwrap,
Undressing me in new ways,
A coming of age.

Walking hand in hand,
You guide me through your city.
Ah, please guide me more.

Beer, cappuccino,
Over dinner we dream dreams.
Heaven and earth meet.

Hidden passages,
New vistas and views galore,
"Thin" places to share.

A slow moonlight stroll,
A taxi-ride to your home.
Two precious children.

An easy visit
Comfortable on your sofa.
Room aglow with warmth.

You gave me a kiss,
Said, "I love you, Lucy Blount!"
I said, "God bless you.

And I love you, too,
But I must add one more word.
I'm in love with you."

That speaks volumes more,
A swimming togetherness,
An intermingling.

Then home to the barn.
Darn, no extra roundabouts.

London to New York

Sitting on the plane,
I love you, Duncan MacLeod.
I don't want to go.

Eyes closed I dream dreams.
I can smell your musky scent.
I can feel your touch.

My hands discover,
My fingers memorize you.
I trace each muscle.

Your smile becomes mine.
Every inch of you I claim,
Marking you with love.

You also marked me.
You brought me into being.
I became alive.

Your eyes penetrate
My mind, my body, my soul
From the very first.

A meltdown occurs.
Timid convent kiss to bliss
In just one short week.

And as for this month
Journeying in Kyros time,
A sense of God's hand.

This be imprinted,
Remembered, celebrated.
We are truly blessed.

Stars and moon stood still.
Never have I heard of such
Synchronicity.

You are delicious.
Double cream and anchovies,
Foreign foods combined.

You're playful and fun,
A boy at heart, then a man,
A virtuoso.

Be completely known
And that will come as it should.
Holy Sacrament.

The walk to Burford,
The walk to Great Barrington,
A pint of lager.

Perfect toasted cheese,
A Kir Royal and peanuts,
Terrible coffee,

Ah, wonderful talks!
A wave-like flow back and forth.
Learning more and more.

Drinking in knowledge.
Listening to every thought,
You, me and me, you,

Playing "Fox and Hounds."
No way could I ever win.
But yet, other ways,

Quick, agile, alive,
I love to watch your mind work.
It shakes and shimmers.

Weaving thoughts galore,
It sparkles with energy,
As do your blue eyes.

Attending a play,
Interesting talks after,
Ever expanding.

Dine at the college,
Enjoying the High Table.
Love seeing you there.

You in your black robe,
A distinguished professor,
Sitting next to me.

I am proud of you,
An admirable profession.
I love watching you.

A Senior Fellow
It was fun glancing your way
And catching your eye.

The plane just landed.
Darn, I'm in New York City.
It's 11:00 p.m.

On to Atlanta,
Then another stop-and-go,
Then to Birmingham.

It's been fun writing.
It's like gazing at a jewel,
Priceless times we've had.

Richer than ever,
Grander than could imagine,
Gloriously fun.

Ah, Dr. MacLeod,
Our journey is beginning.
Pilgrimage takes off.

Soaring down life's road,
Floating over hill and dale,
Walking in tandem.

I just phoned Mama.
She raved over your calling,
I raved over you.

We laughed and giggled.
She senses my happiness.
Ah, all will be well.

Of course it will be.
Could it be anything else?
All is well right now.

Except foot blisters,
Running in the terminals
One gate to the next.

Yes! I made this flight.
Yea, New York to Atlanta
But not homeward bound.

That will happen soon.
You and I will fly away
In less than two weeks.

Can you believe it?
I need to stop this writing.
My brain is slowing.

Slowing, slowing down.
It's been a fun exercise
Revisiting you.

All day long I've dwelled,
Breathing in and out of you,
Relishing each breath.

Smiling on the thoughts,
Twirling your ring with delight,
Seeing you kneeling.

Seeing you smiling.
Sliding it on my finger,
You, lighting my heart.

It does burn brightly.
I rest in the glow of love
As this plane takes off.

I would like a nap!
Yawn, I'll shut my eyes and dream
Of the man I love.

90-minute wait
Until the last plane does leave.
Where will I waltz now?

Which scene revisit?
Your image is everywhere.
You tickle my day.

Your imprint is strong,
It's burned into my psyche.
I'm sealed by your love.

Energy is spent.
It's now 4:30 your time.
Thinking of you helps.

"Let's go have pizza!"
Your children are so precious.
Their welcome means much.

Willing to share you.
We'll be sensitive to them,
Placing no demands.

We'll celebrate them,
Slowly allow love to grow,
Allow, but not push.

I think of my group.
May they not feel abandoned.
It's been so intense.

I'm giving them you.
I'm giving them space to heal,
"A room with a view."

I hope they notice.
Our love is so contagious
It will overflow.

"See, Mom is OK!"
"Better yet, she is in love!"
You go forth now, kids.

It's time to let go.
Embrace the pain and then soar.
It's time for your dreams.

Duncan, you support.
Relinquishing my old world,
Understanding words.

"Ta" for tenderness,
"Ta" for your being with me,
"Ta" for being you.

A profound blessing.
Such a man I've never known.
I stand next to you.

I walk next to you.
I am ready to go forth,
If not, I would drown.

I am swimming free,
Kicking as hard as I can,
About to surface.

A singing mermaid
Turning into a princess,
And you are my prince.

You did not rescue,
That would not have been much fun.
I think the Lord did.

He protected me,
Loosening the tentacles,
Put salve on the hurts.

You continue to.
What a soft embrace you have.
Strong, hard, soft, kind, good.

We're almost landing.
Then the adventure begins,
Explaining ourselves.

Who could do such work?
How can one rationalize
A love miracle?

We'll just pass the peace
Some will get it and some won't
Just like in Taynton.

And that is all right.
The good news is we got it,
Blessed communion.

I love you Duncan.
I thank the Lord God for you.
I yearn to come home.

A Nap at the Barn

Gazing azure eyes
Pierce through my very being,
Drinking all of me.

Enflaming delight,
You are the light of my life,
Husband of all joy.

You kindle my heart.
You blow embers into glow,
Springing the dormant.

Birthing, renewing,
Creating a world unknown,
Reservoirs untapped.

Vibrantly alive,
Touching my heart, soul, body,
Tingling and asking.

I yearn for your touch
In so many different ways,
Love, pinch, nibble, stroke,

Gliding, exploring,
Memorizing all of me
And I learning you.

Muscles, sinews, mind,
Perfectly filling my curves,
Encircling me.

You never binding
But, oddly enough, freeing,
Helping me to soar.

Catching a rainbow.
Into the eternal bliss
Of enfolding arms.

My "Duncan the Cloud,"
I do love you profoundly,
More than life itself.

My world is complete.
Thank you, Lord God, for this man.
My half is now whole.

To Duncan on our Wedding Day
November 16, 2000

May my mind be etched,
Be indelibly printed,
A moment in time.

Exquisitely sweet,
When I am awesomely loved
By Duncan MacLeod.

Thoughtful tenderness,
Subtle insinuative,
A pat on the back.

Profoundly knowing
Ways I do not comprehend,
You sound my being.

As if measuring
All of my depth, height and breadth,
The waters are calm.

Stream, river, ocean,
We're flowing as if a wave,
Together as one.

There is no panic,
No drowning under water,
No sense of rushing.

Just profound movement,
Magnetic magnetism.
We're drawn together.

From the very start
Your glance penetrated me,
Pulling me towards you.

There is grander news.
This force pulls us towards the Lord.
Together, He calls.

Brings us together.
Long Hanborough meets Freeland
At the Assembly.

We will dance towards Him.
This wave of love, may it flow
Towards eternity

When we will walk out
Hand in hand and greet others
On the shore of love.

Betty, Beverley,
Gran, Grandaddy, and Grandma,
Daddy, Bill, M.K.

There will be others
Who have caught the Light of Christ
Recognizable.

Even though unknown,
Sisters and brothers alike
United in love.

Not now, yet later.
Almighty God is in charge,
His timing – perfect!

This Thursday morning,
All I know is this moment.
I have love today!

When I am called Home,
When graduation time comes,
As I walk to shore

Into the expanse,
Glorious infinity
Of God's agape,

I'll drop to my knees
And cry, "Thank You, Lord Jesus,
For dying for me."

He will take my hand.
Looking up into His face,
I will smile hugely.

I will have come Home
To my "Beloved Bridegroom."
But before I stand,

I'll humbly give thanks
For sending me such a man
As "Duncan the Cloud"

Who broadens Lucy,
Stretches my comprehension
To fathomless love.

Husband, I am yours
Now and through eternity.
All I give to you.

Whe

The Wedding and Honeymoon

Jane, Robert, Betty,
Get me to the place on time,
Decorate the car.

An exciting calm
Compels me into your arms.
We meet and we greet.

We sign documents,
Then hand in hand mount the stairs
Into the chamber.

Exchanging our vows,
All seems so holy and right,
Hearts lock together.

A host of ladies,
Magistrate, and witnesses,
All celebrating.

Your tears are a gift.
Mine will come later that night,
When our love is sealed.

Indelibly marked,
You fleshed out Corinthians,
As you do each day.

Kay surprises us,
Green straw hat as her disguise.
Tears, hugs, rose petals.

Perfect conclusion.
She didn't go to Paris
On our honeymoon!

Gifts to the convent.
They are celebrating too.
Champagne, flowers, sweets.

Then home for photos.
Jo does an excellent job,
Poses all around.

A threshold carry,
A unique experience
Never before done.

"Ta." It was so right,
And so was the honeymoon,
Every part of it.

The car and train ride,
Pilgrims Rest and Westminster,
Kir Royal, our drink.

Notre Dame, Cluny,
San Michel and Sacre Coeur,
Walking Gay Paree.

A kissing waiter
Joining our celebration
At the brasserie.

The world seems to smile.
I think it is apparent,
Two people in love.

Gathering of Time

Gathering of time
Pleated like by a needle,
Pulled close together.

Chronos to Kyros,
Twenty-four hours compressed,
Man's timing to God's.

An accordion
First stretching then contracting
As if a bellows

Spirit empowered,
An arrhythmic melody
Sings eternity.

My mind is foggy,
A time warp experience.
My focus is blurred.

Walking in a dream
Unable to awaken,
A "sleeping beauty."

A kiss is given,
Sending me into a trance.
She awoke, I sleep.

A weeping willow
Flows in the breeze as I write.
Other trees stand still.

Yes! It understands
Going at a different pace,
Interpretive dance.

Soaring Songs

Catching the up draft,
Free falling into your arms,
Soaring loop the loops.

Wind beneath our wings,
We glide into a new world
Our Lord does sustain.

Up, down, all around,
We sing our song together,
Parallel duet.

Close your eyes and feel,
Listen to the melody.
Senses come alive.

Breathing in and out,
We're floating harmonically
Into the future.

Horizons unknown,
Boundaries to be pushed and stretched,
New frontiers ahead.

We do imagine
Glorious, exquisite dreams,
Possibilities.

December 24, 2000

Parallel Skiing
(After skiing in Davos, Switzerland)

Parallel skiing,
Flowing, floating down the hill,
A cloud encircles.

We are connected,
A profound intimacy.
You and I are one.

As the mist engulfs,
Others seem to float away,
Drifting out of sight.

A barrier forms.
We are alone, together,
A white curtain drops.

Like a silken sheet
Or a satin bridal gown,
Purity of place.

A virginal ground
Undulating under us,
A frozen ocean.

We're surfing the waves.
There is no depth perception,
Rising then falling.

You lead, I follow.
The movement melts into one,
Dancing down the slopes.

Synchronized motion.
Only perceive each other,
Our world is complete.

Spooning

Enfold, encircle.
You surround me with your love.
I sense your being.

Encircling me,
Enfolding me in your arms,
My world is complete.

Womb-like in your love,
I find a safe place to grow,
A relaxed haven.

Breathing in and out,
Inhaling and exhaling,
Rhythmical, in tune,

A feline purring.
Sun, stars, moon, a gentle rain,
A pristine heaven.

A budding begins.
You move, you touch, I respond.
A flower comes forth.

Beautiful, perfect,
It's exotically simple,
"A pearl of great price."

A sense of God's love,
A taste of His agape,
Fleshed out by your touch.

Humbly, I receive.
It's too rich to comprehend.
Husband, I say "yes."

January 29, 20

Duncan Doodle-Dog to the Rescue!

(but not really)

By

Lucy Dunn MacLeod

(A.K.A. Goo-Goo)

To the Grans

with

Love

"Give thanks to the Lord, for He is good.

His love endures forever."

(Psalm 136:1)

Duncan died.

It makes your Goo-Goo sad.

I know it makes you sad too.

But I want you to know that I'm O.K.

Because:

Duncan loves me

and

Duncan loves you

and

You love Duncan

and

We all love Jesus

and

Jesus loves us all!

That makes us like a big family full of love.

And do you know what?

Real, Christ-like love never ends.

I want you to be O.K. too.

Also,

I do not want you

to be afraid of death.

It is O.K. too.

It is like graduation

or

changing from one classroom to another.

It's a different room,

space or place.

A *better* one,

or

really the *best* one,

because

it means you're even closer

to

Jesus.

I was there when Duncan died.
We were in bed together.
It was 3:00 a.m. and we were
sound asleep.

I woke up
because I heard Duncan
take four deep breaths,
just like
he was getting ready to
swim under the water
at the lake.

He even moved his arms
like he was swimming
in a race,
which I <u>know</u> he won!

Then,
he was still, quiet, at peace.

So was your Goo-Goo!

I knew Duncan was home
with Jesus.

Of course
I do and will *always* miss touching him,
and hugging him, and feeling him.

But I'm still loving him
and I will all my life!

I do and will *always* miss
his gorgeous blue eyes
and
his cowboy beard
and
his soldier-like march
and
his talking and teaching
and
laughing and playing
and
his tenderness,
his thoughtfulness,
his kindness and fun.

But I'm still loving him
and I will all my life!

And then,
someday,
I hope to graduate, too!
...in God's time.

But, what about Duncan Doodle-Dog?

Well, a few days after Duncan died,
your Goo-Goo drove with
Jo and Damian, Duncan's children,
from Monteagle, Tennessee,
to Murfreesboro, Tennessee,
to be sure the plans for
the funeral were O.K.

They were.

We then went to lunch
at a little café
and
after lunch
we went to a shop
to buy birthday flowers
for one of Jo's friends.

While she shopped, I went
straight to a big basket full
of stuffed animals.
They were
all different

shapes
and SIZES.

I would pick one up and hug it
then put it back down
and pick up another one
and hug it and put it
back down.

Hugging stuffed animals
can make you feel better
when you're
tired
or sad
or mad
or glad.
Don't you think?

Anyway, none of them felt or looked
quite right.
But then... but then...
I saw <u>the</u> most adorable

scruffy

COWBOY-LOOKING

bandana-wearing

bearded

slightly slew-footed

<u>DOG</u>

that I ever saw!

So, I picked him up
and sure enough
he felt *just right*.

He made me smile.

He reminded me of Duncan.

So, I hugged him a little longer
and
I showed him to Jo,
then put him back in the
basket.

As we were leaving the shop
with the flowers,
Jo stopped and said,
"I want to buy that stuffed animal for you."

It made my heart sing.

She bought it
and she gave it to me.
I took it
and hugged it in the store
and
hugged it as we walked down the street
and hugged it as we got in our car to drive back home.

As I said, he felt just right.
<u>And</u>, as I said, I like the way he looked too!

As I rode in the car
I decided to give this precious gift
a closer inspection.

I looked at
his long, hairy ears
I looked at
his shiny brown eyes
I looked at
his cute nose and mouth
I looked at
his two hand-like paws
I looked at
his two foot-like paws
I looked at
his green bandana.

Yes! He was just perfect.

Then... I looked at the tag
around his neck.
And do you know what it said?

Duncan Doodle-Dog!
That's his name!
And,
do you know how much he cost?
$20
(which was just the
right amount
for
Duncan and I had a rule:
You could only spend
$20
on a present.)

Duncan Doodle-Dog to the rescue!
(but not really)

No, Duncan Doodle-Dog
is just a stuffed animal.
He is a sweet gift and I will treasure him,
but what I will treasure more
are the memories
of the *real* Duncan.

Your Goo-Goo has been changed
and rearranged
by Duncan's love.

His love reminds me
of Jesus' love

because He is the real Rescuer

because He is our Savior.

And, as I said, I am O.K.
because:
Duncan loves me
and
I love Duncan
and
Duncan loves you
and
you love Duncan
and
we all love Jesus
and

Jesus loves us all!

P.S. "Grateful, Grateful!"

That's what Duncan and I said every night before we went to sleep. We said it because we are grateful to the Lord for each other and for the love that we share. And we are grateful for our many blessings – and that means you!!

God bless you, precious child.
I love you and so does the Lord Jesus!

Love,
Goo-Goo

Grateful... GREATful!

"Ta, Gorgeous"

Junction of Dean Creek and Spotted Bear River

I do not know why
These circumstances happen,
But I do say "yes"

To the pain of life.
Only then is there blessing.
Duncan, I miss you.

Duncan, I want you.
I want to see your blue eyes.
I want to kiss you.

I want to hold you.
I do in my heart, you know.
Always, infinite.

Afraid and fearful
Over time I will forget
Your exquisite love.

That's impossible!
I have been changed, rearranged.
I'm a new person.

That can't be denied.
Your love has imprinted me.
I am beautiful.

You made me that way.
No, it was the Lord's doing.
You fleshed His love out.

Little did I know
You brought me to His banquet,
You showed me His love.

Heart within a heart.
Sensing the part of a whole,
Love within a love.

You celebrate me.
We both are "grateful, grateful."
I celebrate you.

Known as "the love birds,"
We glowed and shined and shimmered,
A complete union.

Loving companion,
My darling friend and partner,
I can sense you now.

In the gentle breeze,
In the birds' song and soaring,
The movement of leaves,

Vibrant, so alive,
Exciting to be near you,
Your questioning mind.

Always the teacher,
Never intimidating,
Just showing the way.

Loved following you,
Your strong back, your arms swinging,
Your powerful smell.

You drew me to you.
You're still drawing me today,
Yearn to be with you.

I know that I am.
It's just that you are boundless.
There're no boundaries.

You're swimming in love,
Enfolded in the Lord's arms.
He's holding you close.

He's holding me too,
It's just a wider expanse.
No, even closer.

We're more intimate.
We are part of the Body,
Communion of Saints.

I did not know it,
Really did not understand.
You brought clarity.

Kalispell, Montana

Mama, I'm O.K.
Do not worry about me.
I'm strongly fragile.

Do you understand?
Wish I had a black armband.
Then people would know.

Truly, I'm O.K.
I'm just a little fractured.
It's just that I hurt.

Will's talking to Jess.
I want to talk to Duncan.
Alright, so I will.

"I'm not miserable.
I will not wallow in pain.
I will honor you.

Dwelling in your love,
By the grace of the dear Lord,
I will live strongly.

Didn't we have fun,
An extraordinary gift?
Thank you, Father God.

How do I love thee?
Dear, You are my heart's desire.
Let me count the ways."

TV is blaring,
It is thundering outside,
Time to go to sleep.

Lord, you are all strength,
You are all delight and light.
"Grateful, Ta, goodnight."

August 31, 200

Saturday morning,
on the plane home from Montana

Wiping the sink out,
Always opening the door,
Putting the seat down.

My mind's memories.
Let's go to Long Hanborough,
An enclosed garden.

Gaze out the window.
I see you coming to me,
My heart beats for joy.

Your raincoat flying,
You have a "Columbo" look.
You enter our home.

We kiss and embrace,
As if youthful teenagers.
We are together.

"We are together!"
That is my proclamation.
It is a deep truth.

I don't understand,
I just know that it is so.
A reality,

Profound mystery.
We are now, as we were then,
As in the future,

Timeless, together,
Intertwined in life and death,
All eternity.

An internal smile,
A seamless situation.
A deep joy abides.

"Back to the future."
You're just around the corner,
"A Circle of Time."

Jump back to our home,
Living in community,
Jo, Damian, us.

A good way to start.
We became a family,
But they gave us space.

We fold and wash clothes,
Tender, shared activities,
We cook and we clean.

Well, just a little.
Marmite, Bovril, and Lapsang,
New tastes tantalize.

"Do you want a drink?"
"Coffee, tea, hot chocolate?
Kir Royal or port?"

Tuna, tomatoes,
Peanut butter and jelly,
Ginger, we prefer.

Cottage "cowboy" pie,
Chocolate biscuit or two,
Almond M & M's.

Excitingly new,
A freshness to everything,
Glorious birthing.

Sit at the table,
We're across from each other,
Breakfast, lunch, dinner.

Stimulating talks,
Like brilliant, bright light, fireworks,
Stimulating thoughts.

Heart, mind, soul, spirit
Composing new melodies.
You stretch all of me.

"Yea, it's a sweats day!"
Little personal hygiene,
Slippers, beard, no bath.

A slow, rhythmic day,
Rugby, snooker, or western,
Kips and naps galore.

In front of the fire,
Does life get any better?
No, I don't think so.

Like a cat purring,
I rest my head in your lap,
Content as can be.

Romantic poetry plus 1001 Nights, Huck Finn, The Hobbitt

Read out loud to me
Your rugby songs and stories
They do mesmerize.

Drifting and dreaming,
Falling more into your heart,
Not under a spell,

No magic potion,
Just the mystery called love.
Time seems to stand still.

The living room calls.
It's lovely to revisit
A gathering place,

For family and friends,
A Christmas celebration,
A grazing table,

Wooden ornaments.
You share precious memories
As we decorate.

We respect the past,
Relive our worlds together.
Then they become one.

Arthur Weeks painting
Like the one Daddy gave me,
A birthday welcome.

An obnoxious child
On the plane, I need your "glare,"
Sitting right behind.

Dogs and children came.
You were like the Pied Piper,
A magnetic force.

It became a joke.
Everywhere we went, they went.
Is the joke on me?

Ah, he's sleeping now,
Tired because I didn't sleep,
Last leg of the trip.

Let's go up the stairs,
A helping pat all the way
I like to receive.

I like to receive.
I like to receive your touch
Any, every way,

Any, every time.
And I like to touch you, too.
Any, every way,

Just learned "T.M.I."
That's "too much information."
I will not share all.

Sweet moments of love.
There're many treasured secrets,
With respect always.

Love, beloved love,
Viral, vital, vigorous,
Exquisite passion,

Always a banquet,
A feast, a festivity,
An agape meal.

August 31, 2002

Saturday night

Coming home is hard.
I want Duncan in the flesh.
Coming home is good.

I sense him strongly.
"Pilgrim's Rest" is a haven.
It's properly named.

We spent our first night
On the way to gay Paree
On our honeymoon.

Now that's a fun place
For my mind to go dancing
And prancing away...

Sunday morning. Home from Montana

Slept like a baby.
Had a most wonderful dream,
Given a treasure,

One to give away.
Joy of deciding to whom,
Ah, what a sweet gift.

I think it was love,
The kind that Duncan gave me.
You must pass it on.

It spreads like wildfire.
Holy Spirit, fall on us,
Kindle and renew.

Now it's time for church.
Always good family time,
All to Your glory.

You are in the pain.
Thank You, Lord, for being there.
I know You weep, too.

Help, I'm trying to
Take up my cross and follow.
It's just so heavy.

Lord Jesus, I know
You are making all things right.
It's all in Your time.

J.W. Marriott in Atlanta

"Panties in a wad."
Lord, may I not take control.
"Knickers in a twist."

Rescued from the mire.
You placed me in Duncan's arms.
Thank You, Lord Jesus.

You make my heart sing,
You give me the gift of love
Unconditional.

There is no rushing.
God's timing is orderly,
"Open sesame."

Window of glory,
Invisible opening,
Your light shineth forth.

Your will does take place.
May I not get in the way,
A stumbling block.

Lord, give me wisdom,
Solomon-like discernment,
Used to Your Glory.

My stomach's in knots,
My shoulder's starting to ache,
Restlessly sleeping.

Don't want to struggle,
Want to be an instrument.
May Your will be done.

May Your glory shine,
May my efforts glorify
You and You alone.

I seek Your face Lord,
Cling to You with all my might.
Only way for me.

I miss Duncan so.
I know, Lord Jesus, You know.
I know You comfort.

Give me the strength, please,
To walk this walk without him.
It's a hard journey.

But, Lord, Yours was, too.
Use me, please, to Your glory.
Then carry me Home.

May I draw closer.
May I keep my eyes on You.
May I keep the faith.

September 6, 2002

At Martha & Jud's spending the night

Little Jud told me,
"I love you greater than space,"
As I read to him.

A wise four-year-old.
It's his sister's first birthday.
Good to be with them.

Hate being single,
Hate being the odd man out,
"What to do with Mom?"

That's not what they say.
It's not how they act either.
It's the way I feel.

It is my problem.
I loved being a couple,
Duncan made me whole.

I felt beautiful,
I did blossom and flourish.
We're still an item.

I carry his name,
I continue to wear rings.
We're whole, not a half.

I'm whole, not a half,
Mrs. Duncan John MacLeod,
A reality.

Don't be pitiful.
A widow is still a wife.
You are being loved.

This moment in time
And for all eternity.
"Shhh! Be still and know."

All is well in Christ,
We are united in Him.
It's as it should be.

September 7, 20

Driving to Birmingham and
at home alone for the first time

Conserve energy,
Enjoy each activity.
You know less is more.

Don't dwell in the past,
Be present to the present.
The Lord meets you here.

And so does Duncan.
The past has been woven in,
It is part of me.

Christ Jesus is here.
Duncan and I are here, too.
We're all together.

I light a candle
To remind me of Your love
And the warmth it gives.

"Fear not, child, fear not.
Lucy, I know you are tired."
The Lord is with me.

He will strengthen me.
"Rest, precious one, rest in Me.
Call upon My Name."

"Abba, Daddy, Lord,
Pick me up and carry me
Next to Your heart, please."

**At the lake on a retreat
"My Name is Lucy"**

My name is Lucy.
I thought my roles defined me.
That's not who I am.

Pride in wifedom gone,
Pride in motherhood remains,
Prideful Granny, too.

Pride in my letters,
Pride in arranging flowers,
Pride in giving talks.

Altar guild and choir,
Often "holier than thou,"
Lord, forgive my pride.

Duncan John MacLeod
Never saw me do my "acts,"
"Dog and pony shows."

He loves my body
And my mind and spirit, yes.
He loves all of me.

Just like Jesus does.
All roles, acts, performances
Flow out of Christ's love.

Only then, worthwhile.
"I'm nothing but by God's grace."
"My Name is Lucy."

September 22, 2002

Sunday at the Lake

Oh, Lord Jesus Christ,
It's not the products that count.
Help me die to self.

Writings, no big deal.
I like to toot my own horn.
Pitiful, Lucy!

Oh, Lord Jesus Christ,
Help me get out of the way,
Help me die to self.

"Love you forever."
All about relationships,
My precious man showed.

Loving connections,
Christ in him and Christ in me,
Joined to make a whole.

One in unity,
That's all that really matters,
Wholeness in Jesus.

Lord, may Your light shine,
Like moon, lightning, and sparklers
All at the same time,

A glorious sight
That You gave to us last night,
Darkness into light.

Oh, Lord Jesus Christ,
May Your Holy Spirit fill,
Help me die to self.

Please shine through me, Lord,
"Twinkle, twinkle little star,"
Hold me in Your arms

Tenderly embrace,
"How I wonder what you are."
Heal my mourning heart.

Fill it with Your love.
"Up above the world so high,"
Fill it with Your light.

Brighten the darkness,
"Like a diamond in the sky."
All to Your glory.

Then may I come Home,
"Twinkle, twinkle little star,"
Eternally dwell.

Next to Duncan, please
"How I wonder what you are."
If it be Your will.

He fleshed out Your love.
A sliver of Your glory
Abides in my heart.

I'm "grateful, grateful!"
"Twinkle, twinkle little star."
Tell him, "Ta, Gorgeous!"   until....

Reflections on the word "Still"

An assigned theme for the Cambridge Poetry Society

But Still
Hello my darling
~ but still
You are my heart's delight
~ but still
You brought me to the banquet table
~ but still
You filled me with your love
~ but still
You made my heart sing
~ but still
"Ta, Gorgeous!"
If only ~
But still,
All is well.

Still

The water is still.
The leaves are still.
My lover is still.
But wait ~
The wind blows,
It enlivens, refreshes, renews.
Resurrection.
Yes, all is well.

Still

Still, ill,
What's going on?
A blue eye shines
For all eternity.

October 4, 2002

Diplomat Hotel, London
"Lullaby" (A Haiku Prayer)

Come, Lord Jesus, come.
Everything flows out of love.
Come, Lord Jesus, come.

Come, Lord Jesus, come.
"Love you just the way you are."
Come, Lord Jesus, come.

Come, Lord Jesus, come.
May all work flow out of love.
Come, Lord Jesus, come.

Come, Lord Jesus, come.
All actions out of love, too.
Come, Lord Jesus, come.

Come, Lord Jesus, come.
An instrument of Your peace.
Come, Lord Jesus, come.

Come, Lord Jesus, come.
Please change me, rearrange me.
Come, Lord Jesus, come.

Come, Lord Jesus, come.
May I say "yes" to Your will.
Come, Lord Jesus, come.

Come, Lord Jesus, come.
May Your wish be my command.
Come, Lord Jesus, come.

Come, Lord Jesus, come.
May inside match my outside.
Come, Lord Jesus, come.

Come, Lord Jesus, come.
What You see is what You get.
Come, Lord Jesus, come.

Come, Lord Jesus, come.
Be totally without guile.
Come, Lord Jesus, come.

Come, Lord Jesus, come.
Your light shine strongly through me.
Come, Lord Jesus, come.

Come, Lord Jesus, come.
Lord, please come abide in me.
Come, Lord Jesus, come.

Come, Lord Jesus, come.
Make my heart Your dwelling place.
Come, Lord Jesus, come.

Come, Lord Jesus, come.
You are welcomed, please enter.
Come, Lord Jesus, come.

Come, Lord Jesus, come.
There're sins and cobwebs galore.
Come, Lord Jesus, come.

Come, Lord Jesus, come.
Dark spaces, nooks and crannies.
Come, Lord Jesus, come.

Come, Lord Jesus, come.
Your Holy Spirit does clean.
Come, Lord Jesus, come.

Come, Lord Jesus come.
Make this abode Your design.
Come, Lord Jesus, come.

Come, Lord Jesus, come.
Fashion me in Your image.
Come, Lord Jesus, come.

Come, Lord Jesus, come.
May I become as You planned.
Come, Lord Jesus, come.

Come, Lord Jesus, come.
I surrender all to You.
Come, Lord Jesus, come.

Come, Lord Jesus, come.
I'm under new Management.
Come, Lord Jesus, come.

Come, Lord Jesus, come.
Please be the Lord of my life.
Come, Lord Jesus, come.

Come, Lord Jesus, come.
Please be the Love of my life.
Come, Lord Jesus, come.

Come quickly ~ Amen

"I Love You Greater Than Space"

Duncan John MacLeod,
"I love you greater than space!"
You fleshed out God's love.

Wholehearted approach,
An incredible imprint,
A totality.

What does love look like?
How do you envision it?
What sight comes to mind?

What exquisite smell?
What extraordinary feel?
What melodic sound?

Think, touch, tantalize,
Explore the impossible.
Dream outlandish dreams.

No boundaries in love,
Infinite and fathomless,
Rainbow sliding ride.

Do you sense the joy?
Do you sense the thrill of it?
Ecstasy in peace.

Do you know a fact?
Love makes you feel beautiful,
Each one of us is.

A God creation,
We are each uniquely made.
Sometimes we forget.

Life dulls our senses,
Experiences can cloud,
Heaviness sets in.

But then, but then love,
Shimmering, shaking, shining,
Comes forth as a dawn.

Light pierces the heart,
Crackling, melting, healing whole.
All is well again.

Creative new birth,
How the Lord means us to be,
Hallowed harmony.

Bouquets blossoming
Come bursting forth with delight,
Flowers flourishing.

"Pah rum pa pum pum."
Drummer Boy song comes to mind.
"Played my best for Him."

He did his best, too.
Positive parallel dance,
Each encouraging.

"Wow, you're wonderful!"
"You are extraordinary!"
"Gosh, you are gorgeous!"

Our world is a dance.
No sense of time, place or space,
Intertwined freedom.

Just there and aware
Of the whole oneness of us,
Complete unity.

The Lord's universe
Is united in a flash,
God's love becomes clear.

Appendix

P.S.   I'd like to end by including two pieces written by
Duncan the last Valentine's Day. We spent the day on a retrea
at Christ Church in Aspen, Colorado. The first is a meditatio
on Mark 14:3-9 which reads:

> 3   "and being in Bethany in the house of Simon the
> leper, as he sat at meat, there came a woman having an
> alabaster box of ointment of spikenard, very precious; and
> she brake the box, and poured it on his head.
> 4   and there were some that had indignation within
> themselves, and said, "Why was this waste of the ointmen
> made?
> 5   for it might have been sold for more than three
> hundred pence, and have been given to the poor." And
> they murmured against her.
> 6   and Jesus said, "Let her alone; why trouble ye her?
> She hath wrought a good work on me.
> 7   For ye have the poor with you always, and whensoeve
> ye will, ye may do them good; but me ye have not always.
> 8   She hath done what she could. She is come aforehan
> to anoint my body to the burying.
> 9   Verily I say unto you, wheresoever this gospel shall be
> preached throughout the whole world, this also that she
> hath done shall be spoken of for a memorial of her."

e were asked to envisage ourselves as one of the participants
 the scene. Duncan chose Simon the Leper. He ended the
ece with the words: "how wonderful to have on my
mbstone:

> He <u>did</u> all he could."

They are.

ne second writing, which I left in his own script, is a love
tter written as if it were from his Father God to him. It might
ke a few readings to decipher his words but, I believe, well
orth the effort.

Love and all joy.

Lucy

A Meditation on Mark 14:3-9
As Experienced by Simon the Leper

By

Duncan MacLeod

Holy Week, 2002, Christ Church, Aspen, Colorado

Not everyone is willing or prepared to come and dine in the house of a leper. But these were all good friends, men and women. And I mean *good* – people who cared for me, and others like me; for the afflicted, whatever their affliction, disease, poverty, or sadness.

It was a convivial evening but, of course, my friend Jesus was usually at the centre of things: wise, compassionate, funny a born teacher.

There was just one disruptive moment. One of the women present came to Jesus, an expensive jar of perfume in her hand. She broke it and poured its contents over Jesus' head – that was when we knew it was expensive.

How thrilled I was! She had just expended a year's wages ($20,000!) giving pleasure to my dearest friend. Why should the rich get all the pleasure and the poor get all the pain? Is not God's creation bountiful enough for all? Why should the poor deny themselves pleasures and luxuries that others take for granted just to buy a second coat or trousers for their child?

No sooner had these thoughts floated across my mind, than I was brought up short by some of my friends and suddenly I felt very guilty. I had noticed them whispering among themselves. Then a couple of them rebuked the woman harshly. How could you waste what could so easily have been sold for the benefit of the poor? I shuddered at my initial

easure – surely these were good-hearted, right-thinking
iends? Think how many could have been sheltered, clothed
nd fed for the price of that reckless act of generosity.

Not for the first time, however, Jesus surprised me – and
em. Leave her alone, he said. He admired her perception, he
inted again that he would die prematurely and that this was
kind of visionary, pre-annointing of the dead. He had more
an once hinted at an early death. She did what she could, he
id. She did what she could. And he emphasized 'did.' There
e always things we <u>can</u> do. But do we do them? She did. She
raised her friend and teacher in the best way she knew, at
eat expense to herself. Her perfume could not solve the
roblem of poverty.

When my good news is preached about, said Jesus, when
y gospel is proclaimed, her action will always be recalled.

I was quietly pleased that my initial reaction to her act
as right after all, although not entirely for the right reasons,
erhaps. My friends accepted the rebuke, though remained
little puzzled about their future priorities. Should they give
l to the poor or was it better to build monuments to God or
ngage in expensive rituals?

I wonder, if they, like me, found solace in the thought that
hatever my actions, if my motives are pure and I act out of
ve – <u>act</u> I say – then how wonderful to have on my
ombstone:

He <u>did</u> all he could.

14.2.2002

St. Valentine's Day.

Duncan, my son,

You have given me the gift of your time all of today. Thank you. But so far is it rather like a gift a child receives at Christmas – the package contains no batteries, without which the gift looks good, but is lifeless. That is not quite true: the batteries are there but you must charge them. How?

Remember what you have encountered this day, the fellowship of fellow-Christians, the leadership & encouragement of Fil Anderson. Remember the varied perspectives on my word revealed in a joint reflection upon them. But above all, remember my Word itself. Remember, that is, my Word made flesh – my Son. Jesus; but also the utterances he made in my name. The gospel of Mark, 14:3-9, should remain for you an inspiration. The perfume-bearing woman "did what she could." Why? She did it out of love for my Son. You, too, must do what you can, & must do it also out of love for my Son.

122

I do not ask the impossible — I ask for nothing beyond your capacity to achieve. Do what you can, out of love, and the others will be changed & your gift to me will come alive & will complete for me the treasure you have initiated this day.

My Son, Jesus, expressed the same wish a little differently to Peter after He had returned from the Cross. John tells the story in his gospel. 'Do you love me? Then feed my sheep.' 'Do you love me? Then feed my lambs.' 'Do you love me? Then feed my sheep.' Do what you can. That woman gave to Jesus the most valuable thing she possessed. Do likewise. You like to say that the most valuable commodity you possess is Time. Then give of that.

Remember: do what you can, and do it out of love.

Love & Blessings,
from your,
Father in Heaven.

Duncan, my son,

You have given me the gift of your time -- all of today. Thank you. But so far is it rather like a gift a child receives at Christmas -- the package contains no batteries, without which the gift looks good, but lifeless. No, that is not quite true: the batteries are there, but you must charge them. How?

Remember what you have encountered this day, the fellow-ship of fellow-Christians, the leadership and encouragement of Fr. Anderson. Remember the varied perspectives on my word revealed in a joint reflection upon them. But above all, remember my Word itself. Remember, that is, my Word made flesh -- my Son, Jesus; but also the utterances he made in my name. The gospel of Mark 14:3-9, should remain for you an inspiration. The perfume-bearing woman "did what she could." Why? She did it out of love for my Son. You, too, must do what you can, and must do it also out of love for my Son.

I do not ask the impossible -- I ask for nothing beyond your capacity to achieve. Do what you can, out of love, and the batteries will be charged and your gift to me will come alive and will complete for me the pleasure you have initiated this day.

My Son, Jesus, expressed the same wish a little differently to Peter after He had returned from the Cross. John tells the story in his gospel. 'Do you love me? Then feed my sheep.' 'Do you love me? Then

ed my lambs.' 'Do you love me? Then feed my sheep.' Do what you
n. That woman gave to Jesus the most valuable thing she possessed.
o likewise. You like to say that the most valuable commodity you pos-
ss is time. Then give of that.

Remember: do what you can, and do it out of love.
Love and blessings,
From your
Father in Heaven

By God's grace, the dance continues ..

uncan John MacLeod

. . . " *Love never ends.* " . . . .

1 Cor. 13:8

ul Pressly McCain

. . . . *because of Jesus*

I Corinthians 13

hough I speak with the tongues of men and of angels, and have not char-
, I am become as sounding brass, or a tinkling cymbal.

And though I have the gift of prophecy, and understand all
ysteries, and all knowledge; and though I have all faith, so that I could
move mountains, and have not charity, I am nothing.

And thought I bestow all my goods to feed the poor, and though I
ve my body to be burned, and have not charity, it profiteth me nothing.

Charity suffereth long, and is kind; charity envieth not; charity vaunt-
h not itself, is not puffed up,

Doth not behave itself unseemly, seeketh not her own, is not easily
rovoked, thinketh no evil;

Rejoiceth not in iniquity, but rejoiceth in the truth;

Beareth all things, believeth all things, hopeth all things, endureth all
lings.

Charity never faileth: but whether there be prophecies, they
all fail; whether there be tongues, they shall cease; whether there be
nowledge, it shall vanish away.

For we know in part, and we prophesy in part.

) But when that which is perfect is come, then that which is in part
all be done away.

When I was a child, I spake as a child, I understood as a child, I
rought as a child; but when I became a man, I put away childish things.

2 For now we see through a glass darkly; but then face to face: now
know in part; but then shall I know even as also I am known.

3 And now abideth faith, hope, charity, these three; but the greatest
f these is charity.

The Holy Bible
King James Version

Additional books written by Lucy Dunn Blount:

Letters to the Precious Group
    illustrated by Mary Barwick

Letters From the Candidate's Wife
    illustrated by Mary Barwick

Lenten Love Letters
    illustrated by Laura Dale Dockery

Lucy What's ~ Her ~ Name (and your name, too!)
    illustrated by Woodie Long

"Lamkins J. Flock, Get Off That Heap!"
    illustrated by Mary Barwick

Additional books written and illustrated by Mary Barwick:

Alabama Angels

Alabama Angels in Anywhere LA

Alabama Angels Join HEMA

Additional books illustrated by Mary Barwick:

Little Girls Have to Sleep Tonight

Anna Page's Book of Poems

About the Author

am nothing, but by the grace of God."

This is the way Lucy Dunn Blount describes herself. She is a letter
iter and a poet. For over 22 years she has been handwriting letters and
etry of Christian encouragement to "Precious Pilgrim." Thus far there
ve been five books published: three for adults, one adult fable, and one
children. **"I Love You Greater Than Space"** is her first published book
poetry. These writings have been featured on her weekday radio
gram, "Living Treasure with Lucy MacLeod," and on the website **www.
ingtreasure.org**. For the last five years Lucy has also been sending out a
bal monthly letter. She hand addresses over 850 envelopes and draws
le hearts around each recipients's name to remind each that he or she
oved by LOVE, *our Father God.*

It has been said that Lucy is without guile. She is transparent. At 64,
r life experiences have been rich and varied. She says it is her heart's
ayer that her transparency allows the *Light of Christ* to shine through
r writings. She says, "There have been ups and downs and all arounds."
rough it all, she proclaims her Lord's abiding love. Her words of hope
all situations and circumstances seem to bathe the reader with "blessed
urance."

Lucy is president of **Precious Pilgrim Ministries** whose mission is
lift up the Name of the Lord Jesus and to encourage His people."

She is married to Dr. Paul Pressly McCain, and has four grown
ildren and eleven grandchildren, who call her "Goo Goo." She lives in
catur, Alabama.